Taschentrainer Englisch

John Stevens

Common Mistakes in English Grammar

Fehlerfrei sprechen und schreiben

Hueber Verlag

Taschentrainer Englisch

ist eine Reihe von Übungsbüchern im kleinen Format für schnelles und bequemes Üben für zu Hause und unterwegs. Mit den Taschentrainern werden Grammatik, Wortschatz und Sprachgebrauch in authentischen Situationen wiederholt, gefestigt und vertieft. Die Reihe ist optimal für das Selbststudium geeignet.

3. 2. 1. | Die letzten Ziffern
2013 12 11 10 09 | bezeichnen Zahl und Jahr des Druckes.
Alle Drucke dieser Auflage können, da unverändert, nebeneinander benutzt werden.
1. Auflage

Redaktion: Heike Birner, Hueber Verlag, Ismaning
Umschlaggestaltung: Parzhuber und Partner, München
Fotogestaltung Cover: wentzlaff/pfaff/güldenpfennig kommunikation GmbH, München
Coverfoto: © Matton Images/StockByte
Zeichnungen: Irmtraud Guhe, München
Layout und Satz: Birgit Winter, Seefeld
Druck und Bindung: Ludwig Auer GmbH, Donauwörth
Printed in Germany
ISBN 978-3-19-107918-5

Inhalt

Vorwort

Liebe Englischlernende,

die *Taschentrainer Englisch* sind ideal für das schnelle und bequeme Lernen zwischendurch. Das kleine, handliche Format passt in jede Tasche. So können Sie jederzeit, zu Hause und unterwegs, Übungen machen.

Der vorliegende Taschentrainer hilft gezielt, typische Grammatikfehler im Englischen zu vermeiden. Alle besonders fehleranfälligen Bereiche der englischen Grammatik werden behandelt, u.a. Present Perfect, Verlaufsform des Verbs, Zukunftsformen, *if*-Sätze, Infinitiv und Gerundium, Modalverben und Präpositionen.
Einen Überblick über sämtliche Themenbereiche und deren Schwerpunkte erhalten Sie durch das Inhaltsverzeichnis auf Seite 3.

In diesem Taschentrainer finden Sie
- über 100 abwechslungsreiche und unterhaltsame Übungen;
- authentische Situationen und Kontexte aus dem Alltags- und Berufsleben;
- einen übersichtlichen Lösungsteil zur Selbstkontrolle;
- ergänzende Erklärungen zu den Grammatikthemen und typischen Fehlern (im Lösungsteil nach dem Symbol ▶).

Der vorliegende Taschentrainer ist als Begleitmaterial für die Kompetenzniveaus A2 bis B1 des Europäischen Referenzrahmens konzipiert. Er eignet sich bestens zur Evaluation, um zu testen, was man gut oder weniger gut beherrscht.

Viel Spaß mit Ihrem Taschentrainer!

Autor und Verlag

A. Einfache Form und Verlaufsform

1. I'm just finishing my lunch.
2. I live in Hameln.
3. A phone call
4. *Have* and *having*
5. They aren't taking a holiday this year.
6. I don't like the sound of all this.
7. Trends
8. It seems very cold.
9. I was still having breakfast.
10. I need a drink.

A1 I'm just finishing my lunch.

Was passt zusammen?

1. I'm
2. Isabella
3. Why do
4. Ronald
5. Does
6. The boss says
7. The train
8. Do

a. he doesn't like the idea.
b. Mike still live in Merrow?
c. is working from home today.
d. they always arrive late?
e. doesn't run on Saturdays.
f. you really believe that?
g. just finishing my lunch.
h. works only part-time. She has kids.

1	2	3	4	5	6	7	8
g							

A2 I live in Hameln.

Unterstreichen Sie die richtige Form.

1. I (a.) am living / (b.) live in Hameln. I've lived there all my life.
2. A friend of ours from Canada (a.) is staying / (b.) stays with us at the moment.
3. (a.) Are you enjoying / (b.) Do you enjoy the party? – Yes, thanks. I (c.) am having / (d.) have a great time.
4. (a.) I am not having / (b.) I don't have lunch in the canteen usually. I nearly always (c.) am bringing / (d.) bring something to eat from home.
5. Jackie (a.) has / (b.) is having a part-time job in a lawyer's office. But she's going to have a baby soon.
6. People (a.) aren't wanting / (b.) don't want to hear bad news. That's why politicians (c.) promise / (d.) are promising heaven on earth.

A3 A phone call

Ergänzen Sie. Zwei Ausdrücke werden nicht benötigt.

arrives • I can see • I don't think so • ~~I'm just walking~~
is just arriving • is shining • It snows • It's snowing • seem

- ◆ Where are you? Are you at the station yet?
- ● Yes, (1.) *I'm just walking* into the station building now.
- ◆ You're late, aren't you?
- ● (2.) ______________________. It's 9.47, and their train is due at 9.49. It might be late because of the weather anyway.
  (3.) ______________________ hard here at the moment.
- ◆ The sun (4.) ______________________ here.
- ● OK, I'm at the arrivals and departures board. A lot of people (5.) ______________________ to be waiting. There are quite a few delays posted, but Ann & Ian's train is on time. Platform 5. Oh, (6.) ______________________ it now. The train (7.) ______________________.

A4 *Have* and *having*

Ergänzen Sie *I have* oder *I'm having*.

1. Sorry, *I have* no time this weekend.
2. ______________ an argument with my internet provider on the other line. I'll call you back.
3. ______________ lunch with Diana next Tuesday.
4. ______________ a really great holiday. The hotel, the beach, the people – all just great.
5. ______________ a party on 10th May. Can you come?
6. ______________ a lot to do this morning.
7. ______________ three children, two boys and a girl.

A5 They aren't taking a holiday this year.

Sortieren Sie die Teile und bilden Sie Sätze. Achtung: Nicht alle Teile werden benötigt!

1. a holiday / aren't taking / don't take / they / this year

   They aren't taking a holiday this year.

2. does / is / mean / meaning / this symbol / what

   ____

3. Joanna / is trying / to lose / tries / some weight

   ____

4. doesn't eat / isn't eating / meat / she

   Ann's a vegetarian. ____________________________

5. is just closing / just closes / the tourist office

   ____

6. closes / earlier / is closing / it / in the winter

   ____

7. gets better / slowly / is getting better / the situation

   ____

8. am not / I / remember / don't / anything / remembering

   ____

A6 I don't like the sound of all this.

Ergänzen Sie die richtige Gegenwartsform.

1. I (not / like) _don't like_ the sound of all this.
2. We (not / know) ________________ why he did it.
3. Ron and Claire (not / speak) ________________ to each other at the moment.
4. Jem (make) ________________ real progress.
5. We (need) ________________ more time.
6. The paperback version (not / cost) ________________ so much.
7. I (not / mind) ________________ what you do.
8. What (you / do) ________________? – I (try) ________________ to repair this door handle.
9. Jan and Ed have split up. Ed (live) ________________ temporarily with me.
10. Temperatures (rise) ________________ worldwide.
11. Who (you / wait) ________________ for?
12. What (this word / mean) ________________?

A7 Trends

Korrigieren Sie.

1. People ~~go~~ ___are going___ on shorter holidays.
2. Winters ~~become~~ ________________ warmer and wetter in many parts of the globe.
3. The price of oil ~~rises~~ ________________ again.
4. More fathers ~~take~~ ________________ time off to care for their children.
5. People ~~worry~~ ________________ about the economy more.
6. Employers ~~give~~ ________________ more short-term contracts.
7. People ~~buy~~ ________________ smaller cars that use less fuel.
8. More and more people ~~live~~ ________________ a second life online.

A8 It seems very cold.

Korrigieren Sie.

1. It is ~~seeming~~ ___seems___ very cold. Is the heating not on?
2. ~~Are you remembering~~ ______________________ what happened?
3. She's very rich. She ~~is owning~~ ________________ six hotels.
4. No, this ~~isn't belonging~~ ______________________ to me.
5. I ~~am not seeing~~ ______________________ what you are trying to say.
6. ~~Were you understanding~~ ________________________ what he just said?

A9 I was still having breakfast.

Korrigieren Sie – falls nötig.

1. They fixed a fault in the computer system so I couldn't work.
   They were fixing a fault in the computer system so I couldn't work.
2. We didn't eat till they arrived.
   We ______________________ till they ________________.
3. We still sat at the table at midnight.
   We ______________________ at the table at midnight.
4. We saw a flash of light, then we heard a loud explosion.
   We _____________ a flash of light, then we _____________ a loud explosion.
5. I listened to music and had headphones on, so I didn't hear anything.
   I _____________ to music and _____________ headphones on, so I _____________ anything.
6. The boss walked in when we discussed his new hairstyle.
   The boss _____________ when we _______________ his new hairstyle.
7. It rained hard, so I decided to take a taxi.
   It _____________ hard, so I _____________ to take a taxi.
8. I still had breakfast when the taxi arrived.
   I ______________________ breakfast when the taxi ____________.

A10 I need a drink.

Übersetzen Sie.

1. Ich brauche etwas zu trinken.

   I need a drink.

2. Es hängt alles davon ab, was es kostet.

   ____

3. Ich arbeite zurzeit von zu Hause.

   ____

4. Ich lerne Spanisch.

   ____

5. Als ich hinkam *(arrive)*, warteten schon über 50 Menschen.

   ____

6. Sie bauen ein neues Hotel.

   ____

7. Normalerweise stehe ich samstags später auf.

   ____

8. Aber heute arbeite ich.

   ____

B. Present Perfect und Vergangenheit

1. I've seen the report.
2. A or B?
3. We went to Amsterdam last weekend.
4. I've seen this film.
5. I've never eaten kangaroo.
6. When did this come?
7. An email
8. Delaying tactics
9. Have you ever ...?
10. Finders, keepers

B1 I've seen the report.

Was passt zusammen?

1. I've
2. I read it
3. Have you
4. The plane has just
5. It
6. We
7. Has
8. Have there

a. met Jack?
b. been any phone calls?
c. anything important happened?
d. last week.
e. left London late.
f. seen the report.
g. landed.
h. were both at the Frankfurt conference.

1	2	3	4	5	6	7	8
f							

B2 A or B?

Was passt: a oder b?

1. The meeting has just (a.) began / (b.) begun.
2. I've never (a.) fell / (b.) felt so good.
3. We (a.) flew / (b.) flown to Chicago, not New York.
4. I've completely (a.) forgot / (b.) forgotten.
5. She's (a.) spend / (b.) spent quite a lot of time in China.
6. We (a.) swam / (b.) swum out to an island.
7. Who (a.) laid / (b.) lay the table?
8. I (a.) laid / (b.) lay down, but I couldn't sleep.

1	2	3	4	5	6	7	8
b							

B3 We went to Amsterdam last weekend.

Streichen Sie den falschen Satz durch.

1. Wir sind letztes Wochenende nach Amsterdam gefahren.
a. ~~We have been to Amsterdam last weekend.~~
b. We went to Amsterdam last weekend.

2. Wir waren noch nie vorher dort.
a. We've never been there before.
b. We were never there before.

3. Wir waren schon einmal in Den Haag.
a. We've been to Den Haag before.
b. We were in Den Haag before.

4. Wir haben auf einem Hausboot gewohnt.
a. We've stayed in a houseboat.
b. We stayed in a houseboat.

5. Es war wunderschön.
a. It's been wonderful.
b. It was wonderful.

6. Wir haben viel gesehen und hatten viel Spaß.
a. We saw a lot and had a great time.
b. We've seen a lot and had a great time.

7. Wir sind in diesem Frühjahr bisher schon zwei Mal verreist.
a. We've been away twice so far this spring.
b. We were away twice so far this spring.

B4 I've seen this film.

Ergänzen Sie wie im Beispiel.

1. I've seen this film.
   ___*I saw it*___ last week with Hugh.
2. I've done this journey many times.
   ____________ for the first time in 2005.
3. We've begun to pack.
   ________________________ yesterday.
4. I've spoken to Jill.
   ____________ to her on Monday.
5. I haven't slept very well.
   ____________ only three hours last night.
6. Jack has shown the visitors round.
   ____________ when they arrived.
7. I've rung the embassy.
   ____________ yesterday too.
8. I've paid the bill.
   ____________ two days ago.
9. Someone has stolen my parking space.
   ____________ on Tuesday too.

B5 I've never eaten kangaroo.

Ergänzen Sie.

decided • didn't • didn't • ~~eaten~~ • had • have eaten
said • tasted • thought • was

Have you ever (1.) *eaten* kangaroo meat? I (2.) ________ some last month when I (3.) ________ on holiday in New South Wales. It (4.) ________ strange, and I (5.) ________ really like it. But I (6.) ________ want to hurt my Australian hosts' feelings, so in true British fashion I (7.) ________ that I (8.) ________ it was "very interesting". I (9.) ________________ worse things before, but I (10.) ________ that next time someone offers me some I will say no.

B6 When did this come?

Ergänzen Sie.

◆ When (1. this / come) *did this come*?
● Someone (2. bring) ________________ it about ten minutes ago.
◆ Why (3. you / not open) ________________ it?
● Because it's addressed to you.
◆ But I (4. not order) ________________ anything from a company called Webspan.
● Maybe you (5. do) ________________, but you (6. forget) ________________.
◆ I (7. be) ________________ very busy lately, but I (8. not become) ________________ that forgetful!

B7 An email

Ergänzen Sie Present Perfect, Vergangenheit oder Gegenwart.

Thank you for your suggestion. I (1. discuss) *have discussed* it with my colleagues and (2. be) ________________ pleased to tell you that we (3. decide) ________________ that we (4. think) ________________ it is a very good idea.

We have been partners for over 10 years now. During this time we (5. have) ________________ some difficult periods, especially since the credit crisis (6. break out) ________________ in late 2008. We (7. always look for) ________________ solutions that (8. serve) ________________ both parties, and feel that you (9. again find) ________________ one which is good for both of us.

B8 Delaying tactics

Ergänzen Sie die passenden Verben im Present Perfect.

be • buy • check • ~~drink~~ • eat • give • give up • read

(1.) *I've drunk* two cups of coffee, (2.) ________________ my emails, and (3.) ________________ the latest news online, (4.) ________________ my plants some water, (5.) ________________ to the canteen and (6.) ________________ and (7.) ________________ a chocolate bar – (8.) ________________ smoking. So I suppose I'll have to start work now ...

B9 Have you ever ...?

Ergänzen Sie die Fragen. Antworten Sie *Yes, I have* bzw. *No, I haven't.*

1. cut
   Have you ever cut your own hair? ______
2. drive
   ______ a sports car? ______
3. drink
   ______ real champagne? ______
4. ride
   ______ a camel? ______
5. buy
   ______ a diamond ring? ______
6. wear
   ______ a fur hat? ______
7. sing
   ______ in a karaoke bar? ______
8. eat
   ______ seaweed[1]? ______

[1]Seetang

B10 Finders, keepers[1]

Ergänzen Sie.

(1. you / ever find) *Have you ever found* a large amount of money in the street? I have. It (2. be) ___________ a few years ago, in a country that shall remain nameless[2], but which I (3. visit) ________________________ many times in my life and which I (4. always love) ________________________ very much. It (5. be) ___________ Eastertime, and we (6. be) ___________ there on a week's holiday. It (7. be) ___________ still cold at home, and we just (8. want) ___________ to get away from the long cold winter. I (9. often dream) ________________________ of spending the winter in a warm southern country, but I (10. never have) _______ _________________ the money, and I don't expect I ever will.

Anyway, I (11. find) ____________ this 100 euro note in the street. I (12. not think) ___________________ it was right to keep it, so I (13. take) _______________________ it to the police. The first problem was that nobody (14. speak) ____________ English, and they (15. have to) ________________________ go and find the local school teacher. I (16. explain) _________________________ to her what had happened, and she (17. interpret[3]) ________________________ for the policeman. He shrugged his shoulders[4] and (18. say) ____________ something I of course (19. not understand) ________________________. The teacher (20. tell) ___________________ me that the policeman (21. not want) ________________________ any bother[5], and I should keep the money. That had never happened to me before, and (22. never happen) ________________________ again since then!

[1]Wer's findet, dem gehört's [2]das ungenannt bleiben soll [3]dolmetschen
[4]zuckte mit den Schultern [5]irgendwelche Scherereien

C. Present Perfect mit *since*, *for* und *how long*

1. *For* or *since*?
2. What's right?
3. We're old friends.
4. How long?

C1 *For* or *since*?

Kreuzen Sie an.

	since	for	
1.	☒	☐	2007
2.	☐	☐	two and a half years
3.	☐	☐	yesterday afternoon
4.	☐	☐	ten hours
5.	☐	☐	ten hours ago
6.	☐	☐	I don't know when
7.	☐	☐	ages
8.	☐	☐	sometime last year
9.	☐	☐	a short while
10.	☐	☐	a short while ago
11.	☐	☐	a long time
12.	☐	☐	as long as I can remember

C2 What's right?

Kreuzen Sie an.

1.	☐	a.	I have lived here for a long time.
	☐	b.	I have lived here since a long time.
2.	☐	a.	How long do you know Mike?
	☐	b.	How long have you known Mike?
3.	☐	a.	She hasn't been really fit ever since she had that accident.
	☐	b.	She isn't really fit ever since she had that accident.
4.	☐	a.	I need some help, just for half an hour.
	☐	b.	I've needed some help, just for half an hour.

C3 We're old friends.

Korrigieren Sie.

1. I ~~know~~ Jim since university.

   I have known Jim since university.

2. Mrs Franzen ~~is~~ ill ~~since~~ three weeks.

   Mrs Franzen ______________ ill ______________ three weeks.

3. How long ~~do~~ you ~~know~~ this?

   How long ______________________________ this?

4. This situation ~~is developing since~~ a long time.

   This situation ______________________________ a long time.

5. Things ~~calm down~~ since Watson ~~has left~~ the company.

   Things ______________ since Watson ______________ the company.

6. The company ~~is~~ active in Asia ~~since~~ over 30 years.

   The company ______________ active in Asia ______________ over 30 years.

7. How long ~~does~~ this problem ~~exist~~?

   How long ______________________________?

8. How long ~~are you~~ with the company?

   How long _____________________ with the company?

C4 How long?

Ergänzen Sie die Fragen wie im Beispiel.

1. live
   How long have you been living here?
2. work
   ______________________________ for this company?
3. drive
   ______________________________ a car like that?
4. learn
   ______________________________ English?
5. wait
   ______________________________?
6. try
   ______________________________ to reach me?
7. sit
   ______________________________ there?
8. train
   ______________________________ for the marathon?
9. plan
   ______________________________ this?

D. Verneinung mit und ohne *do*

1. I'm not ready.
2. A or B?
3. We're in a hurry.
4. Why not?
5. Not a cold climate
6. No, that's not right.
7. I don't ...

D1 I'm not ready.

Was passt zusammen?

1. I'm not
2. I don't
3. I can't
4. I don't have
5. I didn't
6. I haven't
7. I hadn't

a. make Wednesday.
b. done this before.
c. expected to see William there.
d. meet anyone I knew.
e. agree.
f. to be at the meeting.
g. ready.

1	2	3	4	5	6	7
g						

D2 A or B?

Was passt: a oder b?

1. We ... see them again for a long time.
   a) aren't going to   b) don't
2. I ... much sport.
   a) don't   b) don't do
3. I'm sorry, but I ... much English.
   a) don't speak   b) speak not
4. You've misunderstood me. I ... that!
   a) meant not   b) didn't mean

1	2	3	4

D3 We're in a hurry.

Ergänzen Sie wie im Beispiel.

1. We're late.

   But we ____*aren't*____ very late.

2. I know the first man.

   But I ________________ the other one.

3. We walked over twenty miles on the first day.

   But we ________________ so far on the next two.

4. I have plenty of time.

   But I ________________ much money!

5. I've made a mistake.

   I ________________ this kind of mistake for a long time.

6. I can speak a little Spanish.

   But I ________________ any Portuguese.

7. They'll give us something to drink.

   But they ________________ us anything to eat.

8. I do the washing.

   But I ________________ the ironing.

D4 Why not?

Ergänzen Sie.

can't • didn't • don't • haven't • ~~isn't~~ • won't

1. Why *isn't* this stupid machine working?
2. Why __________ this stupid machine do what it's supposed to do?
3. Why __________ I spend a bit more money and buy something that was a bit more reliable?
4. Why __________ I just take it back to the shop and try and change it?
5. Why __________ they write instruction manuals that a normal person can understand?
6. Why __________ they updated the software?

D5 Not a cold climate

Korrigieren Sie – falls nötig.

1. It's not a very wet climate.
   korrekt
2. It rains not often.
   ____
3. We have not many frosts.
   ____
4. You haven't to have a lot of thick coats.
   ____
5. We've not had snow for years.
   ____

D6 No, that's not right.

Sortieren Sie die Teile und bilden Sie Sätze. Jeweils ein Wort wird nicht benötigt!

1. city / don't / I / in / live / not / the

   I don't live in the city.

2. before / ever / happened / hasn't / never / this

   ____

3. didn't / do / I / not / this

   ____

4. coming / don't / Frank / isn't / why

   ____

5. decide / decided / didn't / till / we / yesterday

   ____

6. do / don't / making / more / preparation/ why / you

   ____

7. absolutely / agree / don't / I / not

   ____

8. doesn't / in / passes / Torquay / stop / the / train

   ____

D7 I don't ...

Übersetzen Sie.

1. Ich mag dieses Zimmer nicht.

   ____

2. Wir wissen nicht, was passiert ist.

   ____

3. Er macht keinen Sport.

   ____

4. Zurzeit arbeite ich nicht.

   ____

5. Das ist doch nicht wirklich passiert?!

   ____

6. Ich habe nicht gewartet. Es war spät.

   ____

7. Wir wollten kein Taxi nehmen.

   ____

8. Er hat nicht viel Talent.

   ____

E. Fragen und Frageanhängsel

1. Who are you?
2. A or B?
3. How did you get there?
4. When do we arrive?
5. Questions, questions, questions
6. An interview
7. Which provider?
8. Talking to a lab technician
9. Right?
10. Right again?
11. That surprises me.

E1 Who are you?

Was passt zusammen?

1. Who are
2. What sort of car
3. When does
4. Who
5. Who do
6. What did
7. Why have
8. What colours
9. Which colour

a. the match start?
b. knows the answer?
c. they invited that idiot?
d. are there?
e. has she got?
f. it cost?
g. is best, do you think?
h. you?
i. you know here?

1	2	3	4	5	6	7	8	9
h								

E2 A or B?

Was ist richtig: a oder b?

1. When ... the problem start?
   a) did b) has
2. Who ... the presentation?
   a) did give b) gave
3. What ...? Maybe I can help.
   a) do you need b) need you
4. Which hotel ... for you?
   a) they booked b) did they book

1	2	3	4

E3 How did you get there?

Ergänzen Sie die Frage.

1. ◆ How (get) did you get here?
   ● I came by car.
2. ◆ (like) __________________ Italian food?
   ● Oh yes! I love it!
3. ◆ (take) __________________ anyone with you?
   ● Yes, I'm taking Fran and Megan.
4. ◆ (do) __________________ anything interesting?
   ● Not really. We had a very lazy two days.
5. ◆ What (should / wear) __________________ ?
   ● It doesn't really matter. They're always very informal.
6. ◆ Who (cook) __________________ in your family when you were a kid?
   ● Actually it was mostly my dad.
7. ◆ Who (ask) __________________ when you needed advice?
   ● That was usually my mum.
8. ◆ Who (go shopping) __________________ in your family?
   ● I do!

E4 When do we arrive?

Streichen Sie den falschen Satz durch.

1. Wann kommen wir an?
a. ~~When we arrive?~~
b. When do we arrive?

2. Was bedeutet dieses Wort?
a. What does this word mean?
b. What means this word?

3. Wen kennst du?
a. Who know you?
b. Who do you know?

4. Wie viel muss ich bezahlen?
a. How much do I have to pay?
b. How much do I must pay?

5. Brauchen Sie ein Taschentuch?
a. Do you need a handkerchief?
b. Need you a handkerchief?

6. Wer schreibt die Einladungen?
a. Who is writing the invitations?
b. Who does write the invitations?

E5 Questions, questions, questions

Was passt zusammen?

1. Does Tina know about the meeting?
2. Will you be at Sandra's party?
3. Has the water boiled?
4. Did you get my message?
5. Can you see OK from where you're sitting?
6. Are you ready?
7. Did they reach an agreement?
8. Have the tickets come?

a. Yes, it has.
b. Yes, I did thanks.
c. Almost. Are you?
d. Not really. Can you?
e. No, I won't, I'm afraid.
f. No, I'm afraid they didn't.
g. Yes, they came in this morning's post.
h. Yes, she does.

1	2	3	4	5	6	7	8
h							

E6 An interview

Ergänzen Sie.

- ◆ So where (1. you be) *were you* last night between 10.30 and midnight?
- ● At home, in bed.
- ◆ (2. anyone can) ________________ confirm[1] that? (3. you be) ________________ with anyone?
- ● That's none of your business!
- ◆ It may be in your interest to have a witness[2].
  When (4. you hear) ________________ about the break-in at your office?
- ● This morning. My secretary called me.
- ◆ What time (5. you get) ________________ this call?
- ● I don't know, 8.15, 8.30.
- ◆ (6. he know) ________________ that the company is in serious financial difficulties?
- ● He's my secretary. I don't tell him everything.
- ◆ How long (7. you be) ________________ in debt[3]?
- ● What does all this have to do with the break-in?
- ◆ That's what I am trying to find out.
  What (8. you do) ________________ after you got the call?
- ● I called my insurance company.
- ◆ Why (9. you do) ________________ that?
- ● Because that's what I didn't do the last time the offices were broken into! It was a big mistake.

[1]bestätigen [2]Zeuge [3]verschuldet

E7 Which provider?

Ergänzen Sie die Frage.

1. Which provider (you / use) _do you use_?
2. Which providers (be) ______________ the most popular?
3. How many people (you / interview) ______________ in last month's survey?
4. How many people (come) ______________ to last month's presentation?
5. What (interest) ______________ people most at conferences like this?
6. What (people / like) ______________ about conferences like this?
7. Who (phone) ______________ the police? Was it you?
8. Who else (you / inform) ______________? Did you tell Mr Roberts?
9. Where (you / be) ______________? I've been looking for you everywhere.
10. Where (you / sit) ______________? I didn't see you.

E8 Talking to a lab technician

Ergänzen Sie.

◆ Where (1. you come) *do you come* from?

● The north of England.

◆ And what (2. you do) ________________?

● I'm a lab technician.

◆ What sort of company (3. you work) ________________ for?

● A food manufacturer.

◆ (4. you be) ________________ with them a long time?

● Three years.

◆ (5. it be) _____________ an interesting job?

● It's OK.

◆ (6. you have to) _____________________ study or train a long time to get your qualifications?

● Quite a long time, but I didn't go to university.

◆ (7. you be) __________ married? (8. you have) ________________ children?

● It's no on both of those.

◆ (9. you always live) _________________________ where you live now?

● No, I grew up near London.

E9 Right?

Was passt zusammen?

1. This is a lovely hotel,
2. A Danish company bought it,
3. You speak some French,
4. They haven't decided yet,
5. You can't swim,
6. Reg lives in Horsham,
7. The tyres need replacing,
8. It won't make a lot of difference,

a. don't you?
b. have they?
c. doesn't he?
d. don't they?
e. will it?
f. didn't they?
g. isn't it?
h. can you?

1	2	3	4	5	6	7	8
g							

E10 Right again?

Ergänzen Sie das passende Frageanhängsel.

1. You don't like Phelps, ___do you___?
2. We're going to be late, ______________?
3. It didn't cost as much as last time, ______________?
4. You'll be coming, ______________?
5. John wasn't there, ______________?
6. Gerda always looks so good, ______________?
7. You eat meat, ______________?

E11 That surprises me.

Ergänzen Sie.

1. ◆ We're all rather worried.
   ● *Are you*__________? I don't think there's any reason to be.
2. ◆ I can't believe that robots can do this job.
   ● *Can't you*__________? They can do amazing things these days.
3. ◆ I don't want to go.
   ● ____________________? Whyever not? It's going to be a great event.
4. ◆ She loves anything exotic – oriental, African, Arabic.
   ● ____________________? I hope she eats 'normal' European food, too.
5. ◆ I know this film.
   ● ____________________? I've never seen it before.
6. ◆ They keep asking for more money.
   ● ____________________? Well, I would just refuse.
7. ◆ We ran out of petrol.
   ● ____________________? So how did you get here?
8. ◆ The snow didn't last.
   ● ____________________? So no skiing?

F. Zukunftsformen

1. I'll ...
2. I'll have fish.
3. A or B?
4. All right?
5. More than one option

F1 I'll ...

Korrigieren Sie.

1. ~~Wait, I help you.~~

   Wait, I'll help you.

2. ~~I give you a hand.~~

   ____

3. ~~I lend you the money.~~

   ____

4. ~~I give you a lift.~~

   ____

5. Just a moment, ~~I get Simon for you.~~

   Just a moment, ______________________________

6. ~~He calls you back.~~

   ____

7. ~~I see if she's here.~~

   ____

8. ~~They let you know~~ as soon as possible.

   ______________________________ as soon as possible.

F2 I'll have fish.

Ergänzen Sie.

◆ Are you ready to order?
● I think so. Amy? Have you decided?
■ (1. have) *I'll have* the fish, please.
◆ And what would you like with that? Salad or vegetables?
■ (2. take) ______________ vegetables, please.
◆ And you, sir?
● I think (3. have) ______________ the steak.
◆ Certainly, sir. And how would you like it?
● Medium, please. No, (4. have) ______________ it rare.
◆ Certainly. And what would you like to drink?
● I think (5. we try) ______________ the South African red. Is that OK with you, Amy?
■ Sure.
◆ It's a very nice wine, I can really recommend it. A bottle?
● Yes, please.
■ And (6. we take) ______________ a bottle of mineral water, too.
◆ Sparkling or still?
■ Still, please.
◆ Any starters?
■ (7. not have) ______________ anything, thanks.
● Nor me, thanks. (8. we have) ______________ a dessert instead.

F3 A or B?

Was stimmt: a oder b?

1. a) I expect we meet again in Frankfurt.
   b) I expect we'll meet again in Frankfurt.
2. a) He doesn't want to stay the night because he's leaving on a business trip the next morning.
   b) He will not stay the night because he's leaving on a business trip the next morning.
3. a) I have a feeling that something awful happens.
   b) I have a feeling that something awful is going to happen.
4. a) What do you do this Friday? Do you have time then?
   b) What are you doing this Friday? Do you have time then?
5. a) We don't go away this Christmas.
   b) We're not going away this Christmas.
6. a) We leave the dog with Karen's parents as usual.
   b) We'll be leaving the dog with Karen's parents as usual.

1	2	3	4	5	6
b					

F4 All right?

Kreuzen Sie alle richtigen Lösungen an.

1. When we're in London next month,

- ☐ a. we'll be staying with friends.
- ☐ b. we're going to stay with friends.
- ☐ c. we're staying with friends.
- ☐ d. we stay with friends.

2. The weather forecast doesn't sound too good.

- ☐ a. I expect it rains at the weekend.
- ☐ b. I expect it'll rain at the weekend.
- ☐ c. I expect it's going to rain at the weekend.
- ☐ d. I expect it's raining at the weekend.

3. He's no longer a youngster!

- ☐ a. He'll be 50 next year.
- ☐ b. He'll be being 50 next year.
- ☐ c. He's 50 next year.
- ☐ d. He's going to be 50 next year.

4. How much wine should I get?

- ☐ a. How many people are coming?
- ☐ b. How many people are going to be coming?
- ☐ c. How many people come?
- ☐ d. How many people will be coming?

F5 More than one option

Ergänzen Sie eine passende Zukunftsform.

1. The meeting tomorrow (only be) ____________________ two hours.
2. Maybe there (not be) ____________________ enough time to discuss everything.
3. We (move) ____________________ house next month.
4. This time next week I (lie) ____________________ on the beach.
5. By this time next week we (do) ____________________ most of the work.
6. When (you take) ____________________ your exam?
7. I suppose (you have) ____________________ next Friday off.
8. Maybe the recession (not be) ____________________ as bad as all the experts are forecasting.
9. There's no point in rushing. The train (leave) ____________________ by now.

G. Aktiv und Passiv

1. Record holders etc.
2. Who did it?
3. A or B?
4. From active to passive
5. Tourist questions
6. Who and/or what?
7. Who did it?

G1 Record holders etc.

Ergänzen Sie.

a film • ~~a horror story~~ • a play • a series of children's books

J.K. Rowling • ~~Steven King~~ • Steven Spielberg • William Shakespeare

1. 

a horror story by Steven King

2. 

____

3. 

____

4. 

____

Und nun korrigieren Sie.

Michael Schumacher Steffi Graf

5. The record for tennis Grand Slam singles titles is held ~~from Margaret Court~~.
   It ____________________.

6. The record for Formula 1 championships is held ~~from Juan Fangio~~.
   It ____________________.

G2 Who did it?

Was passt zusammen?

1. Someone has
2. Over 1000 hits
3. We are being
4. Over one million euros have
5. The road was
6. A far higher number of sales had
7. English is
8. Many of these places had not

a. asked to accept pay cuts.
b. been discovered as tourist destinations.
c. widened last year.
d. left a message on the answering machine.
e. been expected.
f. were recorded on the website within the first two hours.
g. been spent.
h. spoken all over the world.

1	2	3	4	5	6	7	8
d							

G3 A or B?

Was passt: a oder b?

1. We ... made to feel very unwelcome.
   a) was b) were
2. 'Yesterday' was a famous song ... the Beatles.
   a) by b) from
3. I couldn't get into the room because it ... .
   a) was being cleaned b) was cleaned
4. Where ...? I seem to recognize that tree.
   a) has this photo been taken b) was this photo taken?
5. Bags ... at reception.
   a) can be left b) can left
6. A new model ...
   a) has just been launched b) is just launched
7. Reminders ... next week.
   a) will be sent out b) will send out
8. A lot of changes ... since then.
   a) are made b) have been made
9. ...
   a) By who was the brochure designed?
   b) Who was the brochure designed by?
10. We ... refreshing cold drinks when we arrived.
    a) were being offered b) were offered

1	2	3	4	5	6	7	8	9	10
b									

G4 From active to passive

Wandeln Sie wie im Beispiel um.

1. Someone has made a serious mistake.
   A serious mistake has been made. __________

2. They'll tell us tomorrow.

   We ____________________ tomorrow.

3. They're still testing the system.
   The system ____________________

4. They didn't invite us.
   We ____________________

5. Someone was filming the event.
   The event ____________________

6. They are re-printing the book.
   The book ____________________

7. They ate up all the food in minutes!
   All the food ____________________ in minutes!

8. Nobody had expected such a huge crowd.
   Such a huge crowd ____________________

9. They are monitoring all phone calls and emails.
   All phone calls and emails ____________________

G5 Tourist questions

Übersetzen Sie.

1. Wann wurde das Schloss errichtet?
   When was the castle built?
2. Wann ist das Hotel eröffnet worden?
   ___
3. Wann werden die Koffer abgeholt (werden)?
   ___
4. Wo sind die Tickets ausgestellt [*issue*] worden?
   ___
5. Wie sind Sie informiert worden?
   ___
6. Wird der Briefkasten heute geleert [*empty*] (werden)?
   ___
7. Warum sind die Betten nicht gemacht worden?
   ___
8. Hat man unsere Bestellung vergessen?
   ___
9. Wird ein Trinkgeld erwartet?
   ___

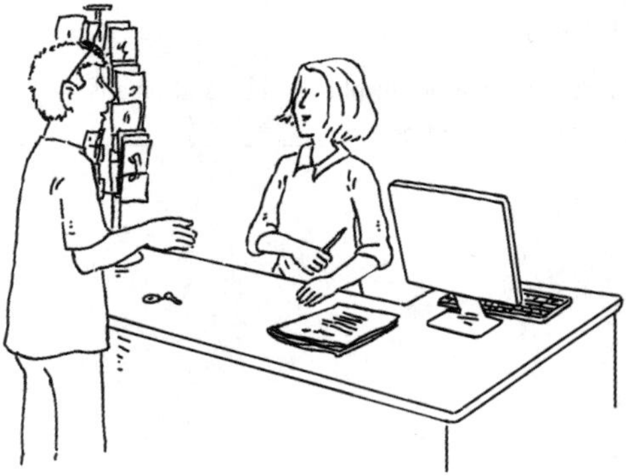

G6 Who and/or what?

Was ist richtig: a, b oder a und b?

1. We had to answer lots of questions.
   a. We were asked lots of questions.
   b. Lots of questions were asked.
2. Someone explained the rules to us.
   a. The rules were explained to us.
   b. We were explained the rules.
3. They offered me help with the removal costs as part of the deal.
   a. Help with the removal costs was offered as part of the deal.
   b. I was offered help with the removal costs as part of the deal.
4. They gave us very little time to make up our mind.
   a. Very little time was given for us to make up our mind.
   b. We were given very little time to make up our mind.
5. They promised me assistance.
   a. Assistance was promised.
   b. I was promised assistance.
6. They suggested that we should re-think the packaging.
   a. It was suggested that we should re-think the packaging.
   b. We were suggested to re-think the packaging.
7. They described the whole process in great detail.
   a. The whole process was described in great detail.
   b. We were described the whole process in great detail.

G7 Who did it?

Ergänzen Sie die Rückfragen, indem Sie das Passiv verwenden.

1. A famous British architect designed the museum.
   Sorry. Who was it designed by ____________________?
2. They've deposited the key with the neighbours.
   Sorry, who ____________________ with?
3. The interim manager will inform the workforce.
   Sorry. Who ____________________?
4. Local business people are sponsoring the event.
   Sorry, who ____________________?
5. The CEO signed the letter.
   Sorry, who ____________________?
6. The company has been taken over by a foreign investor.
   Sorry, who ____________________?
7. Edison invented it.
   Sorry, who ____________________?
8. The government is going to bail the company out[1].
   Sorry, who ____________________?

[1]eine Bürgschaft übernehmen für

H. Infinitiv und Gerundium

1. A or B?
2. Do you enjoy cooking?
3. They aren't taking a holiday this year.
4. Would you like ...?
5. I saw it happen.
6. She accused me.
7. *By, instead, without, ...*
8. What are you afraid of?
9. A or B?

H1 A or B?

Was passt: a oder b?

1. a) I hope to be able to come.
   b) I hope being able to come.

2. a) We've just finished repairing the broken window.
   b) We've just finished to repair the broken window.

3. a) I suggested calling Alexander and asking him.
   b) I suggested to call Alexander and ask him.

4. a) I'd like trying to learn Dutch.
   b) I'd like to try and learn Dutch.

5. a) We've decided to wait.
   b) We've decided waiting.

6. a) I've given up to try.
   b) I've given up trying.

7. a) You can't avoid making mistakes on a project like this.
   b) You can't avoid to make mistakes on a project like this.

8. a) I refuse taking no as an answer.
   b) I refuse to take no as an answer.

9. a) I don't mind paying a bit extra if the quality is good.
   b) I don't mind to pay a bit extra if the quality is good.

10. a) I can't imagine doing your job.
    b) I can't imagine to do your job.

11. a) We're looking forward to see you again.
    b) We're looking forward to seeing you again.

1	2	3	4	5	6	7	8	9	10	11
a										

H2 Do you enjoy cooking?

Ergänzen Sie die richtige Form.

1. ◆ Do you enjoy (cook) ___cooking___ for a big crowd?
   ● Yes, I do. And I like (try out) ______________ new recipes.

2. ◆ Don't do it! You'll risk (make) ______________ an enemy of the man. And that's something you'd regret (do) ______________ till the end of your days.
   ● What would you recommend (do) ______________ then?

3. ◆ We need to practise (do) ______________ this in a hurry.
   ● Yes, we don't want (make) ______________ any mistakes.

4. ◆ Can you remind me (ask) ______________ Jill for the address?
   ● I can't promise (remember) ______________.

5. ◆ It's no use (worry) ______________.
   ● No, you're right. There's no point (get) ______________ anxious.
   ◆ Just stop (worry) ______________ and hope for the best.

6. ◆ I was looking forward to (enjoy) ______________ a nice long lazy weekend. I felt like (stay) ______________ in bed all weekend. But then Martin decided (do) ______________ a blitz on the garden.

H3 They aren't taking a holiday this year.

Sortieren Sie die Teile und bilden Sie Sätze. Achtung: Je ein Teil wird nicht benötigt!

1. badly / behaving / he / liking / seems / to like
   He seems to like behaving badly.
2. a lift / I / giving / offered / them / to give
   ____
3. at the café / don't / me / meeting / mention / to meet
   ____
4. admit / being / I / there / to be
   ____
5. asking for / help / I / really dislike / to ask
   ____
6. can't / carry on / like this / meeting / to meet / we
   ____
7. closing / discussed / the factory in Poland / they / to close
   ____
8. about it / claims / having / he / known / nothing / to have
   ____

H4 Would you like ...?

Korrigieren Sie.

1. ~~Would you like that I help you?~~
   Would you like me to help you?

2. ~~Would you like that we wait for you?~~
   ______________________________ for you?

3. ~~I'd like that you go to the conference for us.~~
   ______________________________ to the conference for us.

4. ~~I want that you completely re-do this.~~
   ______________________________ completely re-do this.

5. ~~Does he really expect that I work every weekend?~~
   ______________________________ every weekend?

6. ~~I need that you pick up the children from school.~~
   ______________________________ the children from school.

7. ~~Would you like that I shut the window?~~
   ______________________________ the window?

8. ~~Do you want that I take Sven to the airport?~~
   ______________________________ Sven to the airport?

9. ~~I'd love that he makes just one mistake.~~
   ______________________________ just one mistake.

H5 I saw it happen.

Unterstreichen Sie die richtige Form.

1. I saw it (a.) happen / (b.) to happen.
2. We've decided not (a.) book / (b.) to book in advance.
3. Just don't let this (a.) happen / (b.) to happen again!
4. Can you get someone (a.) clear up / (b.) to clear up the room?
5. We'd better (a.) leave / (b.) to leave fairly soon because of the traffic.
6. I'll make them (a.) pay / (b.) to pay for this!
7. They won't let me (a.) park / (b.) to park any closer.
8. Did you hear the police cars (a.) pass by / (b.) to pass by?

1	2	3	4	5	6	7	8
a							

H6 She accused me.

Was passt zusammen?

1. She accused me
2. Banks were criticized
3. The protesters were prevented
4. They thanked us
5. I'm very proud
6. There's no real alternative
7. Is there any chance
8. We've had little success

a. from entering the building by the police.
b. of doing it all by myself.
c. to flying. It's too far away.
d. of finding a flat for under 600 euros?
e. of trying to manoeuvre her out of her job.
f. for looking after their cat.
g. in finding a replacement for Sarah Johnson.
h. for lending to people who weren't credit-worthy.

1	2	3	4	5	6	7	8
e							

H7 *By, instead, without, ...*

Wandeln Sie wie im Beispiel um.

1. If you book online, you can save quite a bit. (by)
   You can save quite a bit by booking online.
2. Let's not go on the bus, but let's take a taxi. (instead)
   ______________________ instead of ______________________
3. I asked the question. I didn't even think. (without)
   ______________________ without ______________________
4. If you read a lot, you can improve your vocabulary. (by)
   ______________________ by ______________________
5. Scan the attachment for viruses, then open it. (before)
   Before ____
6. We drove all the way. We didn't stop. (without)
   ______________________ without ______________________
7. I won't have coffee, I'll take tea for a change. (instead)
   Instead ____
8. He invested in the stock market and lost a lot of money. (by)
   ______________________ by ______________________

H8 What are you afraid of?

Ergänzen Sie.

at • for • in • of • on

1. I'm always afraid _of_ making a mistake.
2. I'd be interested _____ finding out more.
3. Sandra's good _____ dealing with this sort of problem.
4. I got tired _____ waiting and left.
5. Are you in favour _____ commissioning an independent review?
6. I don't believe _____ being soft on beginners.
7. Do you have any specific reason _____ asking this?
8. I'm grateful to you _____ informing me so promptly.
9. I'd like to congratulate you _____ making such a good choice.
10. Is there any point _____ continuing with this?

H9 A or B?

Was stimmt: a oder b?

1. a) I must remember calling Janine and ask her how she got on at her interview.	b) I must remember to call Janine and ask her how she got on at her interview.
2. a) Have you forgotten losing our way when we went there the first time?	b) Have you forgotten to lose our way when we went there the first time?
3. a) I forgot paying the bill, and now they've sent a reminder.	b) I forgot to pay the bill, and now they've sent a reminder.
4. a) Don't you remember meeting them in Amsterdam once, quite by chance?	b) Don't you remember to meet them in Amsterdam once, quite by chance?
5. a) I stopped on the way down once to stretch my legs.	b) I stopped on the way down once stretching my legs.
6. a) I've stopped even opening all these junk-mail newsletters.	b) I've stopped even to open all these junk-mail newsletters.
7. a) I meant to ask you: have you got your money back yet?	b) I meant asking you: have you got your money back yet?
8. a) Flying with a budget airline usually means getting up in the middle of the night.	b) Flying with a budget airline usually means to get up in the middle of the night.

1	2	3	4	5	6	7	8
b							

I. *if*-Sätze

1. *If* or *when*?
2. With or without *will*?
3. If I know ...
4. What's wrong?
5. I'll deal with it.
6. If ..., then ...

I1 *If* or *when*?

Ergänzen Sie.

1. I'm meeting Ann next week. ___When___ I see her, I'll tell her what you need.
2. Would it be OK ________ I came a little later?
3. I'll do the plan ________ I have all the data. That should be by tomorrow at the latest.
4. ________ Jonathan agrees, we can borrow his boat.
5. ________ the weather stays fine, we could have a barbecue.
6. ________ it's fine, we often have a barbecue.
7. I don't know what I would do ________ I didn't have you to help me.
8. ________ you get stuck, give me a call.
9. ________ I'm not there, just take a taxi.

I2 With or without *will*?

Unterstreichen Sie die richtige Form.

1. When I sleep in old buildings, I (a.) seem / (b.) will seem to dream more.
2. (a.) We eat / (b.) We'll eat when Jack gets here. He said he'd be here by seven.
3. When I see Mervin, (a.) I check / (b.) I'll check if he's got everything he needs.
4. If they find out, (a.) there's / (b.) there will be hell to pay.

I3 If I know ...

Was passt zusammen?

1. If I know the answer by this evening,
2. What would you have done
3. What will you do
4. They'll be here by six
5. They'd be here by six
6. They would have been here by six
7. What would you do
8. If I knew the answer,
9. If I had known the answer then,

a. if your firm moved its base to another country?
b. if there are no problems with the traffic.
c. if they left at four.
d. if I hadn't warned you?
e. if they hadn't had that breakdown.
f. I'll let you know.
g. if the weather's bad?
h. I wouldn't have to ask you!
i. we would have been saved a lot of trouble.

1	2	3	4	5	6	7	8	9
f								

I4 What's wrong?

Korrigieren Sie.

1. ~~It would be better if I would have more time.~~

   It would be better if I had more time. ______

2. ~~If you will want, I can come back later.~~

   ____________________, __________ come back later.

3. ~~If I would have seen you, I had stopped.~~

   ____

4. ~~It made me feel happier if I would be more prepared.~~

   __________ feel happier, ______________ more prepared.

5. ~~If it wouldn't been cheaper, I didn't buy it from a foreign company.~~

   ______________________________ from a foreign company.

6. ~~Where would you live if you can choose?~~

   ____

7. ~~They hadn't invited me to the meeting if Hannah didn't said somethin~~

   ____________________ to the meeting ______________ something.

8. ~~We fly on a weekday if we would have the choice.~~

   __________ on a weekday __________________ the choice.

I5 I'll deal with it.

Ergänzen Sie die richtige Form.

1. I (deal) will deal with it this weekend if I have time.
2. She says she (be) ______________ back at work on Monday if all goes well.
3. If he had recognized the warning signs, he (not be) ______________ ____________ so surprised at what happened.
4. If you (not drink) ______________ wine in the evenings, you would sleep much better.
5. If Ronald (call) ______________, can you ask him to leave a message, please?
6. What (you / do) ______________________ if they had said there were no places left?
7. If I (have) ______________ their mobile number, I could give them a call.
8. If we (can) ______________ sell our house for a decent price, we might move.
9. Think how much better things would be if everyone (have) ______________ their own room.
10. If I (not see) ______________ it with my own eyes, I (not believe) __________________________ it!
11. If Noel (not go) ______________ to that exhibition, he (never meet) ____________________________ Sophie.
12. If I (not read) ______________ the book, I (not understand) ____________________________ the movie.

I6 If ..., then ...

Übersetzen Sie.

1. Wenn der Bus nicht bald kommt, gehe ich zu Fuß.

   ____

2. Ich hätte nicht ja gesagt, wenn ich Zweifel gehabt *[be in doubt]* hätte.

   ____

3. Ich würde dir helfen, wenn ich wüsste wie.

   ____

4. Wenn er mich noch einmal Fritzi nennt, bringe ich ihn um!

   ____

5. Wenn wir verloren hätten, wäre es nicht das Ende der Welt gewesen.

   ____

6. Es wäre schrecklich, wenn wir das Wetter kontrollieren könnten.

   ____

7. Auch wenn sie es mir schenken würden, würde ich es nicht haben wollen.

   ____

8. Wenn ich die richtige Kleidung mitgenommen hätte, hätte ich nicht die ganze Woche gefroren.

   ____

9. Wenn die Firma nicht diese riskanten Investitionen getätigt hätte, wäre sie nicht bankrott gegangen.

   ____

J. Modalverben

1. Does Bernd have to ...?
2. I can't swim.
3. *Mustn't* or *needn't*
4. Can do!
5. I've been able to contact him.
6. *Have to*
7. All right?
8. *Can*, *may*, etc.
9. A or B?

J1 Does Bernd have to ...?

Was passt zusammen?

1. Does
2. Am
3. Do
4. Are
5. He wasn't
6. It could
7. He must
8. There might not
9. You might have

a. you able to take a day off?
b. be crazy to do that.
c. allowed to ask questions.
d. told me!
e. I allowed to take photos?
f. be time.
g. Bernd have to go to school on Saturdays?
h. happen any time.
i. you have to ask permission?

1	2	3	4	5	6	7	8	9
g								

J2 I can't swim.

Ergänzen Sie.

~~can't~~ • couldn't • might not • mustn't • shall • will • would

1. I'm very embarrassed about the fact that I ___can't___ swim.
2. ____________ I see if he's there?
3. We ____________ be able to come. I'll let you know tomorrow.
4. You ____________ do that! There'll be all hell to pay if they find out.
5. Anna ____________ come because she was away on business.
6. ____________ you agree that this is not the best time to try and sell
7. I just heard the door. That ____________ be Andy.

J3 *Mustn't* or *needn't*

Ergänzen Sie.

1. You ___________ laugh. It's a serious matter.
2. You ___________ hurry. We've still got lots of time.
3. I ___________ forget to take a camera.
4. The Thompsons ___________ worry. Nobody is going to build a supermarket in a neighbourhood like this.
5. Frank and Joel ___________ attend. I know they have more important things to deal with.
6. Something like that ___________ cost a lot of money.

J4 Can do!

Ergänzen Sie das fehlende Wort.

1. Ich kann Französisch.
   I can ______ French.
2. Bitte schreib du die Karte. Du kannst es so gut.
   You write the card please. You can ______ it so well.

J5 I've been able to contact him.

Ergänzen Sie die richtige Form.

could have • ~~couldn't~~ • haven't been able to • wasn't able to • weren't able to • won't be able to

1. I've managed to speak to Jack at last. I *couldn't* get hold of him yesterday.
2. From next week you ______________ park here any more. They're going to start building on the site.
3. I'm still looking for a present. I ______________ find anything suitable yet.
4. We would have loved to stay longer, but we ______________. We had to get back.
5. Sven wasn't at the meeting, so I ______________ ask him.
6. The effects ______________ been much worse. We were very lucky.

had to • ~~will have to~~ • will have to • won't have to

7. It's no good. We *will have to* ask for more time.
8. I ______________ wait over two hours. I was furious!
9. You ______________ be more careful in future.
10. Don't worry. You ______________ say anything.

J6 *Have to*

Korrigieren Sie.

1. I ~~hadn't to~~ wait very long.
   I *didn't have to* wait very long.

2. What ~~have we to~~ do?
   What ____________________ do?

3. When ~~have we to~~ be there?
   When ____________________ be there?

4. Why ~~must you~~ say that? That was stupid.
   Why ____________________ say that? That was stupid.

5. The work ~~mustn't~~ be handed in till Monday.
   The work ____________________ be handed in till Monday.

6. I was really quite surprised. We ~~mustn't~~ show any ID.
   I was really quite surprised. We ________________ show any ID.

7. How long ~~had you to~~ wait?
   How long ____________________ wait?

8. If your flight's at 6.30 tomorrow morning, ~~mustn't~~ you get up very early?
   If your flight's at 6.30 tomorrow morning, ____________________ get up very early?

J7 All right?

Kreuzen Sie alle richtigen Lösungen an.

1. I'm afraid I can't let you in just like that.
   - ▢ a. Can I see your ID, please?
   - ▢ b. Could I see your ID, please?
   - ▢ c. May I see your ID, please?

2. I'm afraid I have to ask you to leave.
   - ▢ a. It isn't allowed to use mobile phones here.
   - ▢ b. You can't to use mobile phones here.
   - ▢ c. You aren't allowed to use mobile phones here.

3. They seem to have changed things.
   - ▢ a. We've never been allowed to park here before.
   - ▢ b. We've never can park here before.
   - ▢ c. We've never could park here before.

4. Where's Jack? He organized this meeting.
   - ▢ a. He can't have forgotten, can he?
   - ▢ b. He can't have forgotten, has he?
   - ▢ c. He mustn't have forgotten, must he?

5. I don't think we can just march in and help ourselves.
   - ▢ a. We had better to ask first.
   - ▢ b. We ought to ask first.
   - ▢ c. We should ask first.

J8 *Can, may,* etc.

Ergänzen Sie in der richtigen Zeitform.

1. Es kann sein, dass sie unsere Pässe sehen wollen.
   They ___________ want to see our passports.
2. Es könnte sein, dass ich nicht komme.
   I ___________ not come.
3. Es kann morgen regnen. Wir wissen es nicht.
   It ___________ rain tomorrow. We don't know.
4. Konnten sie den Fehler finden?
   _________________ find the fault?
5. Musstet ihr etwas unterschreiben?
   _________________ sign anything?
6. Auf diesen Augenblick habe ich lange warten müssen.
   I _________________ wait a long time for this moment.
7. Es darf nicht passieren.
   It _________________ happen.
8. Ich weiß nicht, mit wem sie spricht. Es kann Peter sein.
   I don't know who she's talking to. It ___________ be Peter.

J9 A or B?

Was stimmt: a oder b?

1. a) When you lost your job, it must be very difficult for you.
   b) When you lost your job, it must have been very difficult for you.

2. a) I may can help you. Ask me again tomorrow.
   b) I may be able to help you. Ask me again tomorrow.

3. a) Fantastic. You must be feeling over the moon!
   b) Fantastic. You must feeling over the moon!

4. a) Things could been worse, so I shouldn't complain.
   b) Things could have been worse, so I shouldn't complain.

5. a) To have to sit and watch and not be able to do anything was the hardest part.
   b) To must to sit and watch and not be able to do anything was the hardest part.

1	2	3	4	5
b				

K. Artikel und Begleiter

1. On Monday
2. Twice a month
3. A or B?
4. They argued and argued.
5. I'm a teacher.
6. A or B?
7. St. Pancras Station
8. A friend
9. Love
10. All right?

K1 On Monday

Was passt zusammen?

1. You can tell me when I see you on
2. We meet on the
3. The next meeting is on
4. We meet for
5. We don't meet so often in the
6. There's a break in

a. the second of March.
b. summer.
c. brunch.
d. August.
e. first Saturday in the month.
f. Friday.

1	2	3	4	5	6
f					

K2 Twice a month

Korrigieren Sie.

1. We meet ~~twice in the month~~.
   We meet *twice a month*.
2. Fresh rolls are baked ~~four times in the day~~.
   Fresh rolls are baked ____________________.
3. There's a bus to the local town only ~~twice in the week.~~
   There's a bus to the local town only ____________________.
4. It's the sort of thing that happens ~~once in the lifetime~~.
   It's the sort of thing that happens ____________________.

K3 A or B?

Was stimmt: a oder b?

1. a) Our son is training as a teacher.
   b) Our son is training as teacher.

2. a) My boss is a workaholic.
   b) My boss is workaholic.

3. a) Why are you always in a such hurry?
   b) Why are you always in such a hurry?

4. a) What a beautiful day!
   b) What for a beautiful day!

5. a) What a beautiful weather!
   b) What beautiful weather!

6. a) Tony is a golfer.
   b) Tony is golfer.

7. a) He's a member of several clubs.
   b) He's member of several clubs.

8. a) Please have a seat.
   b) Please take seat.

1	2	3	4	5	6	7	8
a							

K4 They argued and argued.

Was passt zusammen?

1. They argued all weekend, almost without
2. We need to look at the system as
3. What do you do for
4. I haven't seen Amy for
5. Let's just stay at home for
6. Oh dear, what

a. a living?
b. a long time.
c. a whole.
d. a break.
e. a pity.
f. a change.

1	2	3	4	5	6
d					

K5 I'm a teacher.

Übersetzen Sie.

1. Ich bin Lehrerin.
   I'm a teacher.
2. Es war so eine furchtbare Reise.
   ____
3. Was für ein Auto fährt er?
   ____
4. Was für ein herrliches Wetter!
   ____
5. Wir treffen uns einmal im Monat.
   ____

K6 A or B?

Was stimmt: a oder b?

1. a) Where do your children go to school?
   b) Where do your children go to the school?

2. a) They are closing school in Green Street.
   b) They are closing the school in Green Street.

3. a) When was church built?
   b) When was the church built?

4. a) Do people in this country still go to church?
   b) Do people in this country still go to the church?

5. a) At least half the people didn't notice anything.
   b) At least the half of the people didn't notice anything.

6. a) Most people were asleep.
   b) The most people were asleep.

7. a) Who got most the votes?
   b) Who got the most votes?

8. a) It's been like this all week.
   b) It's been like this all the week.

1	2	3	4	5	6	7	8
a							

K7 St. Pancras Station

Ergänzen Sie *the*, wenn es nötig ist.

1. Eurostar trains arrive at __–__ St. Pancras Station.
2. Which river runs through London? Is it ______ Thames?
3. I love ______ Alps.
4. I have no desire to climb ______ Mount Everest.
5. She lives in ______ Half Moon Street.
6. The biggest lake in Africa is ______ Lake Victoria.
7. We land at ______ Gatwick Airport, not Heathrow.
8. My favourite London park is ______ Green Park.
9. Everybody knows ______ Tower Bridge.
10. Where exactly are ______ Ardennes?

K8 A friend

Übersetzen Sie.

1. Tim ist ein Freund von mir.

   ____

2. Andrea ist eine Kollegin von Julia.

   ____

3. Ein Bruder von Jack fährt einen alten Jaguar.

   ____

4. Nachbarn von uns haben ein Haus in Spanien.

   ____

K9 Love

Ergänzen Sie die Übersetzung.

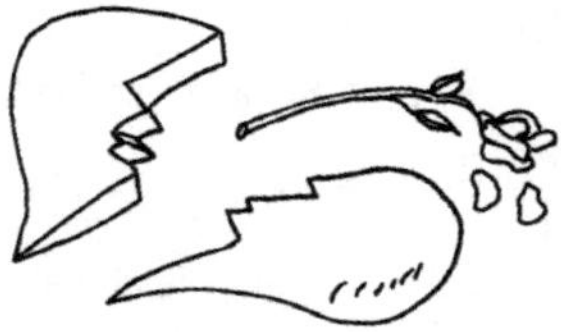

1. Die Liebe hält nie, oder?
   ___Love___ never lasts, does it?

2. Welches Land ist der Geburtsort der Demokratie?
   Which country is the birthplace of ________________?

3. Die Geschichte unserer Stadt begann vor 800 Jahren.
   ________________ of our town began 800 years ago.

4. Es hat mehrere große Präsidenten in der amerikanischen Geschichte gegeben.
   There have been several great presidents in ________________.

5. Das Leben und der Tod gehören zusammen.
   ________________ and ________________ belong together.

6. Wann hast du von dem Tod erfahren?
   When did you hear about ________________?

7. Das Leben ist ein Abenteuer.
   ________________ is an adventure.

8. Wie die Zeit vergeht!
   How ________________ flies!

9. Welche Partei ist nicht für die Freiheit?
   Which party does not stand for ________________?

10. Schau: die Schönheiten der Natur!
    Look: the beauties of ________________!

K10 All right?

Kreuzen Sie alle richtigen Lösungen an.

1.
- ▢ a. I know nearly all people in this room.
- ▢ b. I know nearly all the people in this room.
- ▢ c. I know the people in this room nearly all.

2.
- ▢ a. I know all in our street.
- ▢ b. I know every in our street.
- ▢ c. I know everyone in our street.

3.
- ▢ a. Both skiers were injured.
- ▢ b. Both the skiers were injured.
- ▢ c. The both skiers were injured.

4.
- ▢ a. Neither hotel has any rooms left.
- ▢ b. Neither of the two hotels has any rooms left.
- ▢ c. The hotels have neither any rooms left.

5.
- ▢ a. Nobody of us knew about it.
- ▢ b. None of us knew about it.
- ▢ c. No one of us knew about it.

L. Singular und Plural

1. Boxes
2. A or B?
3. Where are my glasses?

L1 Boxes

Wandeln Sie wie im Beispiel um.

1. What's this box doing here?
   What are these ___*boxes*___ doing here?

2. A new business has been opened.
   Several new ______________ have been opened.

3. Do you have the address?
   Do you have the ______________?

4. Can you make a copy, please?
   Can you make some ______________, please?

5. I don't want a green tomato, I want a ripe one!
   I don't want green ______________, I want ripe ______________!

6. Jason is my brother-in-law.
   Jason and Alan are my ____________________.

7. There's an interesting new series on TV.
   There are several interesting new ______________ on TV.

8. What criterion are you using?
   What ______________ are you using?

9. We have a fox, a mouse and a sheep.
   We have ______________, ______________ and ______________.

10. I have a tooth that's causing problems.
    I have two ______________ that are causing problems.

L2 A or B?

Was stimmt: a oder b?

1. a) We've just received an interesting new information.
   b) We've just received some interesting new information.

2. a) Let me give you an advice.
   b) Let me give you a piece of advice.

3. a) Her hair was a different colour when I saw her last.
   b) Her hairs were a different colour when I saw her last.

4. a) This furniture is old, but comfortable.
   b) These furniture are old, but comfortable.

5. a) The damage was enormous.
   b) The damages were enormous.

6. a) These spaghetti are cold!
   b) This spaghetti is cold!

7. a) It was a difficult task.
   b) It was a difficult work.

8. a) She speaks a very good English.
   b) She speaks very good English.

9. a) Progress is slow.
   b) Progress are slow.

10. a) This room is absolute chaos!
    b) This room is an absolute chaos!

L3 Where are my glasses?

Übersetzen Sie.

1. Wo ist meine Brille?
   Where ___are my glasses___?
2. Wo ist die Polizei?
   Where ______________________________?
3. Ich habe drei Hosen gepackt.
   I've packed three ______________________________.
4. Die USA haben große Probleme.
   The USA ______________ great problems.
5. In Zeiten wie diesen sind sechs Prozent Zinsen viel.
   In times like these six per cent interest ____________ a lot.
6. Die Schere ist auf dem Tisch.
   ____________________ on the table.
7. Die Ware kommt morgen.
   ____________________ coming tomorrow.
8. Die Nachrichten sind gut.
   ____________________ good.
9. Die Treppe ist steil.
   ____________________ steep.

M. Adjektiv und Adverb

1. A or B?
2. *Bad* and *badly*
3. Odd one out
4. *Careful* or *carefully*?
5. Right or wrong?
6. Trends
7. A or B?
8. Here or there?
9. Every day

M1 A or B?

Was passt: a oder b?

1. Have you spoken to Jenny ...?
   a) late b) lately
2. We arrived back very ... yesterday evening.
   a) late b) lately
3. I feel ... tired.
   a) incredible b) incredibly
4. Have you ever seen such an ... performance?
   a) incredible b) incredibly
5. How ... do you know them?
   a) good b) well
6. I hadn't been feeling very ... so I went to the doctor's.
   a) good b) well
7. I was never very ... at maths.
   a) good b) well
8. This sort of weather is ..., even for this part of the world.
   a) extreme b) extremely
9. The service is ... unreliable.
   a) extreme b) extremely
10. It was ... to see some new faces at last.
    a) wonderful refreshingly b) wonderfully refreshing

1	2	3	4	5	6	7	8	9	10

M2 *Bad* and *badly*

Was passt zusammen?

1. I slept
2. I had a really
3. I've never stayed in such a
4. The man in the next room snored
5. At four o'clock there was a
6. It was
7. I felt pretty
8. I complained

a. noisy hotel room.
b. sudden loud noise.
c. badly last night.
d. suddenly there. I don't know what it was.
e. noisily all night long.
f. angrily to the management.
g. bad night.
h. angry.

1	2	3	4	5	6	7	8
c							

M3 Odd one out

Streichen Sie, was nicht passt.

1. quickly – ~~friendly~~ – especially – happily
2. slowly – carefully – well – madly
3. fast – early – hard – happy
4. automatically – basically – ethnically – publicly

M4 *Careful* or *carefully*?

Ergänzen Sie die richtige Form.

careful

1. Listen *carefully* to what I have to say.
2. Be ______________ what you do with that knife.

excited

3. You look ______________. Is something about to happen?
4. We heard a car pull up outside, and Janine looked ______________ out of the window.

particular

5. Was there any ______________ colour you were looking for?
6. The sofa was a ______________ horrid colour.

lovely

7. This tastes ______________.
8. It's a ______________ meal.

anxious

9. ______________ glances passed between them, but neither of them said anything.
10. You seem ______________. What's the matter?

M5 Right or wrong?

Korrigieren Sie den *kursiv* gedruckten Teil, falls nötig.

1. Three people arrived *early*, nobody arrived late.
   korrekt
2. You are very *good informed*.
3. In this sort of job you really have to work *hardly*.
4. His first wife died *tragicly* in a car accident.
5. The country has a *goodly* developed economy.
6. It was *hardly* necessary to point out Ferrow's mistake yet again.
7. The children are all very *good behaved*.
8. He's a very *good-natured* dog and would never bite anyone.

M6 Trends

Korrigieren Sie.

1. Sales are much ~~badder~~ ______________ than in the same period last year.
2. They are 20% ~~more low~~ ______________.
3. It's not getting ~~easyer~~ ______________ to make forecasts.
4. Things were much ~~more better~~ ______________ ten years ago.
5. We've sold the ~~lest~~ ______________ number of units in our luxury range.
6. They are of course much ~~expensiver as~~ ________________________ mass-market models.
7. The downturn has come much ~~sooner as~~ ______________ expected.
8. Many of my colleagues are much ~~more surprised as I~~ ______________________________.
9. They don't have the same kind of overview ~~like I~~ ________________________.
10. This is not the ~~most easyest~~ ______________ business to be in in a time of crisis.

M7 A or B?

Was passt: a oder b?

1. a) You must always be prepared!
   b) You must be prepared always!

2. a) I usually am ready first.
   b) I am usually ready first.

3. a) We don't often watch TV.
   b) We don't watch often TV.

4. a) She drinks never alcohol.
   b) She never drinks alcohol.

5. a) I had an accident yesterday.
   b) I had yesterday an accident.

6. a) I'm still waiting for a reply.
   b) I'm waiting still for a reply.

7. a) They've announced just some job losses.
   b) They've just announced some job losses.

8. a) I do every day the same. It's so boring.
   b) I do the same every day. It's so boring.

9. a) She's flying next week to Trinidad.
   b) She's flying to Trinidad next week.

10. a) There probably won't be enough time.
    b) There won't probably be enough time.

1	2	3	4	5	6	7	8	9	10
a									

M8 Here or there?

Markieren Sie die richtige Stellung.

1.	(easily)	We can (a.) _X_ reach (b.) ____ Chicago by nightfall.
2.	(slowly)	The rain (a.) ____ is (b.) ____ starting to clear.
3.	(usually)	The process (a.) ____ doesn't take (b.) ____ this long.
4.	(certainly)	I (a.) ______ don't (b.) ______ agree.
5.	(rapidly)	He (a.) ______ found (b.) ______ a replacement.
6.	(eventually)	I (a.) ______ got (b.) ______ to sleep.
7.	(soon)	You'll (a.) ______ forget (b.) ______ the whole thing.
8.	(soon)	You'll (a.) ______ have forgotten (b.) ______ the whole thing.

M9 Every day

Übersetzen Sie.

1. Ich nehme jeden Tag meine Medizin.

   ____

2. Ich sehe dich wahrscheinlich bald wieder.

   ____

3. So ein altes Auto kaufe ich nie wieder!

   ____

4. Sie verließ vor zehn Minuten das Büro.

   ____

N. Präpositionen

1. A or B?
2. *At, in* or *on*?
3. Not before lunch
4. A or B?
5. Right or wrong?
6. A or B?
7. In my opinion
8. I'm tired of it.
9. A, B, C or D?

N1 A or B?

Was stimmt: a oder b?

1. a) Brighton is at the coast.
   b) Brighton is on the coast.

2. a) There wasn't a cloud at the sky.
   b) There wasn't a cloud in the sky.

3. a) Everest is the highest mountain in the world.
   b) Everest is the highest mountain of the world.

4. a) Is the Dead Sea below sea level?
   b) Is the Dead Sea under sea level?

5. a) Who were you at the phone with for so long?
   b) Who were you on the phone to for so long?

6. a) Come and sit beside me.
   b) Come and sit besides me.

7. a) What are you doing at Christmas?
   b) What are you doing on Christmas?

8. a) We'll be by Janet's parents at Christmas Day.
   b) We'll be with Janet's parents on Christmas Day.

1	2	3	4	5	6	7	8

N2 *At, in* or *on*?

Ergänzen Sie.

1. I suggest we meet _at_ the entrance.
2. The party is _____ Jane's house.
3. I shall be _____ the office all day.
4. The company's headquarters are _____ 17 Spring Gardens.
5. _____ the weekend I like to get out of town.
6. They have a cottage _____ the country.
7. There's somebody _____ the door.
8. There were some expensive-looking prints _____ the wall.
9. I've spent the whole day _____ my computer.
10. I shall be _____ a conference in Bilbao next week.
11. How much time do you spend ____ the internet?
12. Who's the person _____ this photo?
13. Mason is _____ the doctor's. He's not feeling well.
14. I had to stop _____ the traffic lights.
15. Actually I hate lying _____ the beach.

N3 Not before lunch

Ergänzen Sie.

1. I'll meet you _____ lunch, not before.
2. We'll see you _____ Monday.
3. When there is a full moon, it's not really dark _____ night.
4. I sometimes sit next to her _____ lunch.
5. What are you doing _____ 1st May?
6. Isn't your birthday _____ June?
7. I haven't spoken to him _____ last week.
8. It happened while I was _____ work.
9. What's _____ TV tonight?
10. Have you always lived _____ this address?
11. I would love to live _____ the sea.
12. My office is _____ the third floor.
13. I have no time _____ the moment, I'm afraid.
14. I moved here _____ the age of 12.
15. I've lived here now _____ over 20 years.

N4 A or B?

Was stimmt: a oder b?

1. a) We should get to the airport by ten past seven.
   b) We should get to the airport till ten past seven.
2. a) I waited by seven o'clock, but he didn't call back.
   b) I waited till seven o'clock, but he didn't call back.
3. a) I have to finish this by Monday evening.
   b) I have to finish this till Monday evening.

N5 Right or wrong?

Korrigieren Sie den *kursiv* gedruckten Teil, falls nötig.

1. The opening ceremony is *at 10.30 in the morning.*
   korrekt
2. He usually has the children *on the last Saturday in the month.*
   ____
3. I'm sure the topic will come up sometime *while the meeting.*
   ____
4. It all happened *for several years.*
   ____
5. It should arrive *till Tuesday* at the latest.
   ____
6. I'll be here *up to at least eight.*
   ____
7. We should know *within the next week.*
   ____
8. We live *nearby Oxford.*
   ____

N6 A or B?

Was stimmt: a oder b?

1. Von wem ist das Buch? Kenne ich den Autor?
   a) Who is the book by?
   b) Who is the book from?
2. Wir sind alle gegen den Vorschlag.
   a) We are all against the suggestion.
   b) We are all contra the suggestion.
3. Wie viel Wein sollten wir pro Person einplanen?
   a) How much wine should we plan per person?
   b) How much wine should we plan pro person?
4. Es wurde wegen des Wetters verschoben.
   a) It was postponed because the weather.
   b) It was postponed because of the weather.
5. Es kommt auf die Chefin an. Sie entscheidet.
   a) It's on the boss. She decides.
   b) It's up to the boss. She decides.
6. Wir erwarten bis zu 500 Personen.
   a) We're expecting until 500 people.
   b) We're expecting up to 500 people.
7. Es kann nicht bis morgen warten.
   a) It can't wait by tomorrow.
   b) It can't wait till tomorrow.
8. Ich muss bis morgen eine Antwort haben.
   a) I have to have an answer by tomorrow.
   b) I have to have an answer till tomorrow.
9. Sie bauen sowohl Fabriken als auch Hotels.
   a) They build factories as well as hotels.
   b) They build factories as well than hotels.

N7 In my opinion

Ergänzen Sie.

about • above • at • besides • except • ~~in~~ • of • on (2x) • to

1. ___In___ my opinion this is all going to cost too much.
2. Everyone was there ______ Tina, who was on holiday.
3. We are ahead ______ schedule, which is absolutely fantastic!
4. How much do visitors spend ______ average?
5. If I don't get there ______ time, start without me.
6. According ______ Mr Watkins this is "absolutely normal".
7. I'm calling ______ the email you sent.
8. I'm having to do Pia's job ______ my own.
9. It's ______ all the cost that is worrying me.
10. There were ______ least 80 applicants for the job.

N8 I'm tired of it.

Ergänzen Sie.

1. We got tired ___of___ going to the same place every year.
2. You're very good ______ explaining things.
3. The city is famous ______ its museums.
4. But it's always crowded ______ tourists.
5. What are you interested ______?

N9 A, B, C or D?

Markieren Sie die richtige Antwort.

1. Who do you know here ... Alice?
   a. apart from   b. beside   c. except   d. next to
2. We live ... Hamburg.
   a. by   b. in the near of   c. near   d. nearby
3. I have no intention ... letting you go off with all our knowhow.
   a. at   b. for   c. of   d. on
4. What's the point ... arguing?
   a. at   b. in   c. on   d. to
5. I'm really very proud ... you.
   a. at   b. in   c. of   d. on
6. They accused me ... stealing the code.
   a. at   b. for   c. from   d. of
7. I'll let you know well ... advance.
   a. at   b. by   c. in   d. on
8. We've sold way ... what had been forecast.
   a. ahead   b. beyond   c. more   d. up

0. Dies und das

1. Relative clauses
2. A or B?
3. Indirect speech
4. A, B or C?
5. A or B?

01 Relative clauses

Kreuzen Sie alle richtigen Lösungen an.

1. Who is the guy ...?
   - ☐ a. I saw you with
   - ☐ b. that I saw you with
   - ☐ c. which I saw you with
   - ☐ d. who I saw you with

2. 2300 were sold, ... were later returned.
   - ☐ a. 110 of that
   - ☐ b. 110 of which
   - ☐ c. of that 110
   - ☐ d. 110 of those

3. The teacher ... class gets the best exam results wins an award.
   - ☐ a. of who
   - ☐ b. of who's
   - ☐ c. who's
   - ☐ d. whose

02 A or B?

Was stimmt: a oder b?

1. a) I used to live in Frankfurt.
   b) I used to living in Frankfurt.

2. a) He didn't use to have a beard, did he?
   b) He didn't use to having a beard, did he?

3. a) He claimed kids these days are not used to work hard.
   b) He claimed kids these days are not used to working hard.

4. a) I'm slowly getting used to get up at 4.
   b) I'm slowly getting used to getting up at 4.

03 Indirect speech

Wandeln Sie im Beispiel um.

1. "Teresa called."
   Raymond told me that Teresa _called / had called_.
2. "We won't have time."
   Jacob insisted that ____________________.
3. "I'm leaving tomorrow."
   On Saturday she said that ____________________.
4. "Please take a seat."
   She asked me ____________________.
5. "Has Rebecca been invited?"
   Tony wanted to know ____________________.
6. "Do you speak Portuguese?"
   They asked me ____________________.
7. "I'm so excited."
   He said that ____________________.
8. "They aren't expecting us."
   Sheila was worried that ____________________.
9. "I've made a mistake."
   He knew that ____________________.
10. "Will James be there?"
    She wondered ____________________.

04 A, B or C?

Markieren Sie die richtige Antwort.

1. We're ... outside the station.
   a. meeting b. meeting ourselves c. meeting us
2. They've known ... for a very long time. *[sich]*
   a. each other b. them c. themselves
3. I'd like to introduce ... .
   a. I b. me c. myself
4. Do you have your passport with ...?
   a. you b. your c. yourself
5. Quiet! I can't ... .
   a. concentrate b. concentrate me c. concentrate myself
6. I heard footsteps behind ... .
   a. I b. me c. myself
7. Everyone will have to look after ... . *[sich selbst]*
   a. him and her b. themself c. themselves

05 A or B?

Was stimmt: a oder b?

1. The company has lost sight of (a.) it's / (b.) its customers.
2. This suitcase seems to have lost (a.) it's / (b.) its owner.
3. Oh no, (a.) it's / (b.) its raining again.
4. I don't think (a.) it's / (b.) its a pity.
5. What can you tell me about the building and (a.) it's / (b.) its histo
6. I feel (a.) it's / (b.) its time to finish.

Lösungen

A. Einfache Form und Verlaufsform

A1 2. h 3. d 4. c 5. b 6. a 7. e 8. f

A2 1. b 2. a 3. a, c 4. b, d 5. a 6. b, c

> ▶ **Verlaufsform (mit -*ing*):** eine gerade ablaufende Tätigkeit, eine vorübergehende Situation, eine noch nicht abgeschlossene Entwicklung.
> **Einfache Form:** Dauerzustand oder Gewohnheit.
> Verben, die einen Zustand, d.h. keine Tätigkeit ausdrücken, können nicht in der Verlaufsform stehen.

A3 2. I don't think so. 3. It's snowing 4. is shining 5. seem 6. I can see 7. is just arriving

A4 2. I'm having 3. I'm having 4. I'm having 5. I'm having 6. I have 7. I have

> ▶ ***have*** drückt Tätigkeit aus: kann in der Verlaufsform stehen.
> ***have*** drückt Zustand aus: kann nur in der einfachen Form stehen.

A5 2. What does this symbol mean? 3. Joanna is trying to lose some weight. 4. She doesn't eat meat. 5. The tourist office is just closing. 6. It closes earlier in the winter. 7. The situation is getting better slowly. 8. I don't remember anything.

A6 2. don't know 3. aren't speaking 4. is making 5. need 6. doesn't cost 7. don't mind 8. are you doing? am trying 9. is living 10. are rising 11. are you waiting 12. does this word mean

A7 2. are becoming 3. is rising 4. are taking 5. are worrying 6. are giving 7. are buying 8. are living

> ▶ Noch nicht abgeschlossene Entwicklungen: Verlaufsform

A8 2. Do you remember 3. owns 4. doesn't belong 5. don't see 6. Did you understand

> ▶ Verben, die einen Zustand ausdrücken: keine Verlaufsform

A9 2. korrekt 3. were still sitting 4. korrekt 5. was listening; korrekt 6. korrekt; were discussing 7. was raining; korrekt 8. was still having; arrived

A10 2. It all depends (on) what it costs. 3. I'm working from home at the moment. 4. I'm learning Spanish. 5. When I arrived, over 50 people were (already) waiting. 6. They are building a new hotel. 7. Normally I get up / I normally get up later on Saturdays. 8. But I'm working today.

B. Present Perfect und Vergangenheit

B1 2. d 3. a 4. g 5. e 6. h 7. c 8. b

B2 2. b 3. a 4. b 5. b 6. a 7. a 8. b

▶ begin, began, begun; feel, felt, felt; fall, fell, fallen; fly, flew, flown; forget, forgot, forgotten; spend, spent, spent; swim, swam, swum; lay, laid, laid *(legen, decken)*; lie, lay, lain *(liegen)*

B3 Richtig: 2. a 3. a 4. b 5. b 6. a 7. a

▶ Bericht über ein in der Vergangenheit abgeschlossenes Geschehen (oft mit Zeitbestimmung der Vergangenheit): nur einfache Vergangenheit möglich.
Present Perfect: Etwas hat sich irgendwann in der Vergangenheit ereignet, der genaue Zeitpunkt ist unbekannt oder unwichtig; wichtig ist das jetzige Ergebnis.
Vergangenheitsform: Etwas geschah zu einem bestimmten Zeitpunkt. – **Present Perfect:** Wichtig ist allein die Tatsache, dass sich etwas ereignet hat.

B4 2. I did it 3. We began 4. I spoke 5. I slept 6. He showed them round 7. I rang it/them 8. I paid it 9. Someone/They stole it

B5 2. had 3. was 4. tasted 5. didn't 6. didn't 7. said 8. thought 9. have eaten 10. decided

B6 2. brought 3. didn't you open *[damals, als es gekommen ist]* / haven't you opened *[es ist jetzt nicht geöffnet]* 4. haven't ordered *[es liegt keine Bestellung vor]* / didn't order *[gab keine Bestellung auf]* 5. did 6. have forgotten *[du weißt es jetzt nicht mehr]* / forgot *[nachdem du es tatest]* 7. have been 8. haven't become

▶ Bisweilen sind zwei Sichtweisen auf ein Geschehen möglich – als Ereignis zu einem bestimmten Zeitpunkt in der Vergangenheit (einfache Vergangenheitsform), oder als Ereignis irgendwann in der Vergangenheit mit einem jetzigen Ergebnis (Present Perfect).

B7 2. am 3. have decided *[jetziges Ergebnis]* / decided *[Entschluss zu einem bestimmten Zeitpunkt]* 4. think 5. have had *[in der ganzen Zeit bis jetzt]* 6. broke out 7. have always looked for *[in der ganzen Zeit bis jetzt]* 8. serve / have served / served 9. have again found *[jetziges Ergebnis]*

B8 2. I've checked 3. I've read 4. I've given 5. I've been 6. I've bought 7. (I've) eaten 8. I've given up

B9 2. Have you ever driven 3. Have you ever drunk 4. Have you ever ridden 5. Have you ever bought 6. Have you ever worn 7. Have you ever sung 8. Have you ever eaten

B10 2. was 3. have visited 4. have always loved 5. was 6. were 7. was 8. wanted 9. have often dreamt/dreamed 10. have never had 11. found 12. didn't think 13. took 14. spoke 15. had to 16. explained 17. interpreted 18. said 19. didn't understand 20. told 21. didn't want 22. has never happened

C. Present Perfect mit *since, for* und *how long*

C1 2. for 3. since 4. for 5. since 6. since 7. for 8. since 9. for 10. since 11. for 12. for

C2 1. a 2. b 3. a 4. a

▶ Zum Ausdruck eines Zustandes, der in der Vergangenheit begonnen hat und bis jetzt andauert, verwendet das Englische das Present Perfect, NICHT eine Gegenwartsform, oft zusammen mit *since* (+ Anfangszeitpunkt) und *for* (+ Zeitspanne) bzw. in Fragen mit *how long*.

C3 2. has been, for 3. have you known 4. has been developing 5. have calmed down, left 6. has been active, for 7. has this problem existed 8. have you been

C4 2. How long have you been working
3. How long have you been driving
4. How long have you been learning
5. How long have you been waiting?
6. How long have you been trying
7. How long have you been sitting
8. How long have you been training
9. How long have you been planning

▶ Mit der Verlaufsform des Present Perfect wird das ununterbrochene Andauern eines Vorgangs betont.

D. Verneinung mit und ohne *do*

D1 2. e 3. a 4. f 5. d 6. b 7. c

D2 1. a 2. b 3. a 4. b

D3 2. don't know 3. didn't walk 4. don't have 5. haven't made 6. can't speak 7. won't give 8. don't do

D4 2. won't 3. didn't 4. don't 5. can't 6. haven't

D5 2. It doesn't rain often. 3. We don't have ... 4. You don't have to have ... 5. korrekt

D6 2. This hasn't ever happened before. 3. I didn't do this. 4. Why isn't Frank coming? 5. We didn't decide till yesterday. 6. Why don't you do more preparation? 7. I absolutely don't agree. 8. The train doesn't stop in Torquay.

D7 1. I don't like this room.
2. We don't know what('s) happened.
3. He doesn't do any sport.
4. I'm not working at the moment.
5. That didn't really happen! / ..., did it? 6. I didn't wait. It was late.
7. We didn't want to take a taxi.
8. He doesn't have / hasn't got much talent.

E. Fragen und Frageanhängsel

E1 2. e 3. a 4. b 5. i 6. f 7. c 8. d 9. g

E2 1. a 2. b 3. a 4. b

E3 2. Do you like 3. Are you taking 4. Did you do 5. What should I wear? 6. Who cooked 7. Who did you ask 8. Who goes shopping

▶ *Who* ist Subjekt des Fragesatzes: keine Umschreibung mit *do*.
Who ist Objekt: Umschreibung.

E4 Richtig: 2. a 3. b 4. a 5. a 6. a

E5 2. e 3. a 4. b 5. d 6. c 7. f 8. g

E6 2. Can anyone 3. Were you 4. did you hear 5. did you get 6. Does he know 7. have you been 8. did you do 9. did you do

E7 2. are 3. did you interview 4. came 5. interests 6. do people like 7. phoned 8. did you inform 9. were you 10. were you sitting

E8 2. do you do 3. do you work 4. Have you been 5. Is it 6. Did you have to 7. Are you 8. Do you have 9. Have you always lived

E9 2. f 3. a 4. b 5. h 6. c 7. d 8. e

E10 2. aren't we 3. did it 4. won't you 5. was he 6. doesn't she 7. don't you

> ▶ Bejahter Satz – verneintes Anhängsel (ggfs. *don't / doesn't / didn't* ergänzen). Verneinter Satz – bejahtes Anhängsel.

E11 3. Don't you? 4. Does she? 5. Do you? 6. Do they? 7. Did you? 8. Didn't it?

> ▶ „Echo-Fragen": Bejahter Satz – bejahte Frage. Verneinter Satz – verneinte Frage. In beiden Fällen ggfs. *do(n't) / does(n't) / did(n't)* ergänzen.

F. Zukunftsformen

F1 2. I'll give you a hand. 3. I'll lend you the money. 4. I'll give you a lift. 5. I'll get Simon for you. 6. He'll call you back. 7. I'll see if she's here. 8. They'll let you know

> ▶ Bei spontanen Entscheidungen, Angeboten und Zusagen: *will*

F2 2. I'll take 3. I'll have 4. I'll have 5. we'll try 6. we'll take 7. I won't have 8. We'll have

F3 2. a 3. b 4. b 5. b 6. b

> ▶ Gegenwartsformen, um die Zukunft auszudrücken, sind im Englischen seltener als im Deutschen. Unterschiede zwischen den Zukunftsformen:
>
> - *will*: neutrale Form, ohne Färbung durch Absicht, Plan o.ä. (Beachten Sie: Deutsch „will" = Engl. *want to*)
> - *going to:* Es besteht die Absicht, etwas zu tun; oder die Gewissheit, dass etwas passieren wird.
> - Verlaufsform der Gegenwart: Etwas ist geplant, vorgesehen, abgemacht.
> - Einfache Gegenwart: Etwas ist bestimmt durch Fahr- oder Ablaufplan.
> - Verlaufsform der *will*-Zukunft: Etwas ist so vorgesehen, wird sich so ergeben.

F4 1. a, b, c 2. b, c 3. a, c, d 4. a, b, d

F5 1. will only be / is only going to be 2. won't be / isn't going to be 3. are moving / are going to move / will be moving 4. will be lying 5. will have done 6. are you taking / do you take / are you going to take / will you take / will you be taking 7. you'll have / you'll be having / you're having / you're going to have 8. won't be / isn't going to be 9. will have left

▶ Vollendete Zukunft (Nrn. 5, 9): *will have* + Partizip Perfekt

G. Aktiv und Passiv

G1 2. a series of children's books by J.K. Rowling 3. a film by Steven Spielberg 4. a play by William Shakespeare 5. It is held by Margaret Court. 6. It is held by Michael Schumacher.

G2 2. f 3. a 4. g 5. c 6. e 7. h 8. b

G3 2. a 3. a 4. b 5. a 6. a 7. a 8. b 9. b 10. b

G4 2. will be told 3. is still being tested 4. weren't invited 5. was being filmed 6. is being re-printed 7. was eaten up 8. had not been expected 9. are being monitored

G5 2. When was the hotel opened? 3. When will the bags/suitcases be collected? 4. Where were the tickets issued? 5. How were you informed? 6. Will the letterbox / postbox be emptied today? 7. Why haven't the beds been made? 8. Has our order been forgotten? 9. Is a tip expected?

G6 1. a + b 2. a. 3. a + b 4. b 5. a + b 6. a 7. a

▶ Bei vielen englischen Verben kann das indirekte Objekt eines Aktivsatzes zum Subjekt eines Passivsatzes gemacht werden. Ausnahmen: *explain, suggest, describe.*

G7 2. has the key been deposited 3. will the workforce be informed by 4. is the event being sponsored by 5. was the letter signed by 6. has the company been taken over by 7. was it invented by 8. is the company going to be bailed out by

H. Infinitiv und Gerundium

H1 2. a 3. a 4. b 5. a 6. b 7. a 8. b 9. a 10. a 11. b

▶ In *look forward to* ist *to* Präposition, deshalb folgt ein Gerundium.

H2 1. trying out / to try out 2. making, doing, doing 3. doing, to make 4. to ask, to remember 5. worrying, in getting, worrying 6. enjoying, staying, to do

H3 2. I offered to give them a lift. 3. Don't mention meeting me at the café. 4. I admit being there. 5. I really dislike asking for help. 6. We can't carry on meeting like this. 7. They discussed closing the factory in Poland. 8. He claims to have known nothing about it.

H4 2. Would you like us to wait 3. I'd like you to go 4. I want you to 5. Does he really expect me to work 6. I need you to pick up 7. Would you like me to shut 8. Do you want me to take 9. I'd love him to make

H5 2. b 3. a 4. b 5. a 6. a 7. a 8. a

H6 2. h 3. a 4. f 5. b 6. c 7. d 8. g

H7 2. Let's take a taxi instead of going on the bus. 3. I asked the question without even thinking. 4. You can improve your vocabulary by reading a lot. 5. Before opening the attachment, scan it for viruses. 6. We drove all the way without stopping. 7. Instead of having coffee I'll take tea for a change. 8. He lost a lot of money by investing in the stock market.

H8 2. in 3. at 4. of 5. of 6. in 7. for 8. for 9. on 10. in

H9 2. a 3. b 4. a 5. a 6. a 7. a 8. a

▶ *remember/forget:* für Vergangenes: *-ing*-Form; für Zukünftiges: Infinitiv (jeweils vom Erzählzeitpunkt aus gesehen).
stop (aufhören) und *mean* (bedeuten): *-ing*-Form;
stop (anhalten) und *mean* (vorhaben): Infinitiv.

I. *if*-Sätze

I1 2. if 3. when 4. If 5. If 6. When 7. if 8. If 9. If

I2 1. a 2. b 3. b 4. b

I3 2. d 3. g 4. b 5. c 6. e 7. a 8. h 9. i

I4 2. If you want, I can 3. If I had seen you, I would have stopped. 4. It would make me ... if I was 5. If it hadn't been cheaper, I wouldn't have bought it 6. Where would you live if you could choose? 7. They wouldn't have invited me ... if Hannah hadn't said 8. We would fly ... if we had

I5 2. will be 3. wouldn't have been 4. didn't drink 5. calls 6. would you have done 7. had 8. could 9. had 10. hadn't seen, wouldn't have believed 11. hadn't gone, would never have met 12. hadn't read, wouldn't have understood

I6 1. If the bus doesn't come soon, I'll walk. 2. I wouldn't have said yes if I had been in doubt. 3. I would help you if I knew how to. 4. If he calls me Fritzi again, I'll kill him. 5. If we had lost, it wouldn't have been the end of the world. 6. It would be terrible if we could control the weather. 7. Even if they gave it (to) me, I wouldn't want it. 8. If I had taken the right clothing/clothes with me, I wouldn't have frozen all week. 9. If the firm/company hadn't made these risky investments, it wouldn't have gone bankrupt.

J. Modalverben

J1 2. e 3. i 4. a 5. c 6. h 7. b 8. f 9. d

J2 2. Shall 3. might not 4. mustn't 5. couldn't 6. Would 7. will

J3 1. mustn't 2. needn't 3. mustn't 4. needn't 5. needn't 6. needn't

▶ *mustn't* = nicht dürfen; *needn't* = nicht müssen

J4 1. speak 2. do

J5 2. won't be able to 3. haven't been able to 4. weren't able to 5. wasn't able to 6. could have 8. had to 9. will have to 10. won't have to

J6 2. do we have to 3. do we have to 4. did you have to 5. doesn't have to 6. didn't have to 7. did you have to 8. won't you have to

J7 1. a + b + c 2. c 3. a 4. a 5. b + c

J8 1. may / might 2. might 3. may / might 4. Were they able to 5. Did you have to 6. have had to 7. mustn't 8. may / might

J9 2. b 3. a 4. b 5. a

K. Artikel und Begleiter

K1 2. e 3. a 4. c 5. b 6. d

K2 2. four times a day 3. twice a week 4. once in a lifetime

K3 2. a 3. b 4. a 5. b 6. a 7. a 8. a

K4 2. c 3. a 4. b 5. f 6. e

K5 2. It was such a terrible journey. 3. What kind/sort of car does he drive? 4. What glorious weather! 5. We meet once a month.

K6 2. b 3. b 4. a 5. a 6. a 7. b 8. a

K7 2. the 3. the 4. - 5. - 6. - 7. - 8. - 9. - 10. the

K8 1. Tim is a friend of mine. 2. Andrea is a colleague of Julia's. 3. A brother of Jack's drives an old Jaguar. 4. Neighbours of ours have a house in Spain.

K9 2. democracy 3. The history 4. American history 5. Life and death 6. the death 7. Life 8. time 9. freedom 10. nature

K10 1. b 2. c 3. a + b 4. a + b 5. b

L. Singular und Plural

L1 2. businesses 3. addresses 4. copies 5. tomatoes, ones 6. brothers-in-law 7. series 8. criteria 9. foxes, mice and sheep 10. teeth

L2 1. b 2. b 3. a 4. a 5. a 6. b 7. a 8. b 9. a 10. a

L3 2. are the police 3. pairs of trousers 4. has 5. is 6. The scissors are 7. The goods are 8. The news is 9. The stairs are

M. Adjektiv und Adverb

M1 1. b 2. a 3. b 4. a 5. b 6. b 7. a 8. a 9. b 10. b

M2 2. g 3. a 4. e 5. b 6. d 7. h 8. f

M3 2. well (einziges ohne *-ly*) 3. happy (einziges, das nicht als Adjektiv und Adverb die gleiche Form hat) 4. publicly (einziges, das nicht auf *-ically* endet)

M4 2. careful 3. excited 4. excitedly 5. particular 6. particularly 7. lovely 8. lovely 9. Anxious 10. anxious

M5 2. well informed 3. hard 4. tragically 5. well developed 6. korrekt 7. well behaved 8. korrekt

M6 1. worse 2. lower 3. easier 4. better 5. least 6. more expensive than 7. sooner than 8. more surprised than me / than I am 9. as me / as I have 10. easiest

M7 2. b 3. a 4. b 5. a 6. a 7. b 8. b 9. b 10. a

M8 2. b 3. a 4. a 5. a 6. a 7. a 8. a

M9 1. I take my medicine every day. 2. I'll probably see you again soon. 3. I'll never buy such an old car again! 4. She left the office ten minutes ago.

N. Präpositionen

N1 1. b 2. b 3. a 4. a 5. b 6. a 7. a 8. b

N2 2. at 3. at / in 4. at 5. At / *(AE:)* On 6. in 7. at 8. on 9. at 10. at 11. on 12. in 13. at 14. at 15. on

N3 1. after 2. on 3. at 4. at 5. on 6. in 7. since 8. at 9. on 10. at 11. by 12. on 13. at 14. at 15. for

N4 1. a 2. b 3. a

N5 2. korrekt 3. during the meeting 4. several years ago 5. by Tuesday 6. korrekt 7. korrekt 8. near

N6 1. a 2. a 3. a 4. b 5. b 6. b 7. b 8. a 9. a

N7 2. except 3. of 4. on 5. on 6. to 7. about 8. besides 9. above 10. at

N8 2. at 3. for 4. with 5. in

N9 1. a 2. c 3. c 4. b 5. c 6. d 7. c 8. b

0. Dies und das

01 1. a + b + d 2. b 3. d

02 1. a 2. a 3. b 4. b

03 2. they wouldn't have time 3. she was leaving / would be leaving the next day 4. to take a seat 5. if/ whether Rebecca had been invited 6. if I spoke / speak Portuguese 7. he was so excited 8. they weren't expecting us 9. he had made a mistake 10. if/whether James would be there

04 1. a 2. a 3. c 4. a 5. a 6. b 7. c

05 1. b 2. b 3. a 4. a 5. b 6. a